* THE ILLUSTRATED BOOK OF *
Ballet Stories

AURORA AND HER PRINCE
CELEBRATE THEIR WEDDING IN
THE SLEEPING BEAUTY

THE ILLUSTRATED BOOK OF
Ballet Stories

Written by
BARBARA NEWMAN

Illustrated by
GILL TOMBLIN

With an Introduction by
DARCEY BUSSELL

DORLING KINDERSLEY
LONDON • NEW YORK • STUTTGART • SYDNEY

www.dk.com

Managing editor *Anna Kruger*
Managing art editor *Peter Bailey*
Project editor *Fran Jones*
Art editor *Joanna Pocock*
Production *Kate Oliver*
Picture research *Cynthia Hole*
DTP designer *Nicola Studdart*

First published in Great Britain in 1997
by Dorling Kindersley Limited,
9 Henrietta Street, London, WC2E 8PS
Paperback edition published in 1999
2 4 6 8 10 9 7 5 3 1

Copyright © 1997 Dorling Kindersley Limited, London
Text copyright © Barbara Newman

A CIP catalogue record for this book is available from
the British Library

ISBN 0-7513-7172-6 (paperback alone)
0-7513-6298-0 (paperback with tape)

Colour reproduction by Colourscan
Manufactured in China by Imago

✳ Contents ✳

ODETTE AND SIEGFRIED IN SWAN LAKE

✻ Introduction ✻

A SCENE FROM
SWAN LAKE

WELCOME TO THE TIMELESS world of ballet. I never tire of performing the classical ballets, which combine wonderful fairy-tale stories with magical music, and I have enjoyed dancing in all five of the ballets featured in this book.

If I had to choose a favourite ballet it would be *Swan Lake*. Not only was it my first classical ballet, performed at the age of 20, but I was also fortunate enough to receive coaching from Margot Fonteyn. In this ballet, it is always a challenge to dance the very different characters of Odette and Odile in one evening. I find that the mood of the music brings out the contrast between the White Swan and the Black Swan and helps to define these roles.

All the ballets described in this book are more than one hundred years old. I am sure they will continue to weave their magic and go on entertaining for many more years. I hope you will enjoy them as much as I do.

PREPARING FOR A PERFORMANCE
Classical ballets are known for their strenuous and technical choreography. In order to feel confident performing these ballets, a dancer must devote a lot of rehearsal time to them. This allows you to build up the stamina and strength to enjoy dancing these roles.

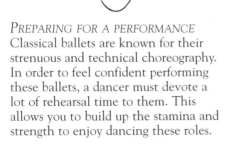

MY ROLE MODEL
I have tried to incorporate the best work of many great dancers into my performances. However, if there is one quality I admire most it is the ability to bring a magic and glow to the stage in every ballet. Nobody did this better than Margot Fonteyn.

GISELLE
In *Giselle*, there is only one interval for your character to change from a young country girl, carefree and happy with life, to a broken-hearted spirit. I love the challenge of the choreography; it offers the chance to achieve the impossible – moving across the stage looking as though you haven't even touched it.

DANCING PARTNERS
Working with a partner requires complete trust. To be an excellent partner you must have strength, confidence, and the ability to know both your partner's role and your own. This allows the most complex lifts to look graceful and simple.

ODETTE/ODILE IN SWAN LAKE
When I first performed *Swan Lake*, I gained most enjoyment from dancing the Black Swan (Odile), given the evil and seductive power that she has. I now find that the quieter strength and the lyrical nature of the White Swan (Odette) is just as exciting to portray.

THE SLEEPING BEAUTY
This is one of the most strenuous ballets for the female lead. Knowing what you have to achieve places such pressure on the dancer that your nerves nearly stop you from making your first entrance. After the difficult Rose Adagio, the weight lifts from your shoulders and you can enjoy the rest of the performance.

✳ Ballet Basics ✳

BALLERINAS AND BEGINNERS WEAR PINK SATIN SHOES

BALLET DANCERS ARE THE SAME all over the world. They wear the same clothes in the studio and practise the same steps, often in the same order. Dancers never stop studying, and all of them, from young beginners to world-famous professionals, return to the classroom day after day to perfect their movements. Dancing is hard work, but the ability to move lightly and gracefully transforms every young dancer into a shining star.

DARNING POINTE SHOES
To keep the stiff tips, or blocks, of pointe shoes from slipping on the floor, dancers create a rough surface on them by darning them in a spiral or in several rows of tiny stitches.

Hair is pulled back and pinned neatly to the head.

The hands should be relaxed and elegant.

Elbows should be gently rounded.

Leotards fit snugly to define the body.

Clean cotton T-shirt

Boys' tights are usually black cotton or nylon.

Rehearsal tutus of stiff tulle move the way a real costume does.

Cotton socks look neat and let the skin breathe.

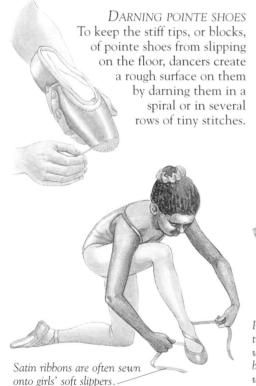

Satin ribbons are often sewn onto girls' soft slippers.

Practice tights, traditionally pink for women, were once silk but are now made of washable, durable nylon.

MAKING SHOES SECURE
Dancers must always feel confident that their shoes will not come off. To anchor them firmly they sew elastic across each shoe from side to side. Ribbons that wrap and tie around the ankle make the shoes even more secure.

The toes of pointe shoes are stiffened inside with layers of shellac and darned outside with tough thread.

Boys wear black or white leather slippers.

THE BASIC POSITIONS OF THE ARMS AND FEET

THE POSITIONS OF THE ARMS
Arm positions are an important part of ballet. They accompany every movement of the body and legs, and must be practised carefully. These five basic positions may be taught with slight variations in different schools.

Elbows should never form a sharp angle.

FIRST POSITION
The arms are placed down and in front of the body, with the little fingers lightly touching the thighs.

SECOND POSITION
The arms are opened and held to the side in a soft curve, with the wrists turned so the palms face slightly forward.

The inside of the forearm should face the front.

The relaxed fingers are clearly separated.

THIRD POSITION
One arm extends to the side, as in second position, while the other curves low in front of the dancer's body.

FOURTH POSITION
One arm is held above the head and slightly forwards, so the dancer can see her own palm. The other extends to the side.

FIFTH POSITION
The dancer holds both arms over her head and far enough in front of her body that she can see her own palms.

THE POSITIONS OF THE FEET
All movements of the feet and legs begin and eventually end in one of these positions. They are the basic alphabet of ballet, and must be practised until they feel easy and completely natural.

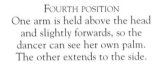

FIRST POSITION
The heels touch and the legs rotate outwards from the hip until the feet make a straight line.

SECOND POSITION
The feet are turned outwards in a straight line and separated from each other by the length of a single foot.

THIRD POSITION
One turned-out foot is placed in front of the other with the front heel touching the middle of the back foot.

FOURTH POSITION
One turned-out foot rests in front of the other, separated from it by the length of one foot. Heels and toes should form a square.

FIFTH POSITION
One turned-out foot is tightly closed against the other. Neither big toe should extend past the opposite heel.

DEMI-PLIÉ

The knees turn out and push directly over the toes.

The heels do not leave the floor.

GRAND PLIÉ

As the knees bend further, the body sinks lower.

The heels leave the floor at the last moment.

PLIÉ
A basic exercise that increases turnout and builds strength in the feet and legs, the *plié* begins every class. A *demi-plié* is a small knee bend, and a *grand plié* is a deep knee bend.

Barre

BACK
(DERRIÈRE)

SIDE
(À LA SECONDE)

FRONT
(DEVANT)

BATTEMENT TENDU
This simple movement, sliding one foot away from the body and back to its original position, warms and stretches the feet. It usually follows the *pliés* as the second exercise at the barre. Like all exercises, it must be done by both the right and left foot.

The Sleeping Beauty

The fantastic ballet, *The Sleeping Beauty*,
is based on a French fairy tale by
Charles Perrault. Marius Petipa
choreographed the ballet, and Peter Ilyich
Tchaikovsky composed the music. The first
performance was given by the Imperial
Ballet at the Maryinsky Theatre,
St Petersburg, Russia in 1890.

The Sleeping Beauty
AT THE CHRISTENING

THE ROYAL INVITATION
Catalabutte, the first character to appear on stage, is in charge of the celebration. He assures the queen that everyone has their invitation.

GUESTS AND GIFTS
Each fairy has a present for the baby. The Candid Fairy brings purity; the Flowing Fairy gives dancing and happiness; the Breadcrumb Fairy promises Aurora will be a happy mother. The Singing Canary gives singing and laughter; the Lively Fairy gives a sparkling personality. The Lilac Fairy brings the gift of wisdom.

Carabosse appears from nowhere in her rumbling black coach. Her ghastly face glows with anger and evil.

ONCE UPON A TIME a princess was born in a kingdom far away. The king and queen decided to name their daughter Aurora, and they invited all the fairies of the kingdom to attend her royal christening at the palace.

One by one the fairies arrived in the great hall to present their splendid gifts to the baby and her proud parents. But just as the Lilac Fairy approached the cradle, black shadows filled the room and the castle shook with thunder. An uninvited guest, the evil fairy Carabosse, swept into the hall in a billowing cloud of smoke. "Why was I not invited to the christening?" she screeched at the quaking king and queen. "I will have my revenge for this cruel insult. I, too, will give your precious daughter a gift."

A horrible curse leapt from her mouth. "Aurora will grow into a beautiful girl," Carabosse sneered, "but one day she will prick her finger on something sharp. And the moment she pricks her finger, she will die."

A crowd of rats surrounds Carabosse. They are her servants and loyal subjects.

The sobbing queen begged Carabosse to change her mind, but the evil fairy only laughed in her face. Luckily, the Lilac Fairy had not yet given the baby her gift of wisdom. Stepping forward, she silenced Carabosse's hideous cackling with a sweet spell of her own.

"Here is my gift," she said gently. "Aurora will indeed grow up, prick her finger, and collapse. But she will not die. Instead she will fall into a deep sleep that will last until a handsome prince kisses her. Only then will the spell be broken."

Overpowered by the Lilac Fairy's loving gift, Carabosse vanished from the scene with a furious hiss. The hall grew bright again as the guests clustered around the cradle to admire the baby princess.

DANGER – CARABOSSE
The evil fairy is often performed by a man (Anthony Dowell) wearing a long dress and elaborate make-up. At the première in 1890, the roles of both Carabosse and the Bluebird were danced by Enrico Cecchetti.

A soft pillow seems to lie between the dancer's arms.

MIME: SLEEP
The language of mime lets dancers speak to each other and to the audience without a word. For "sleep" the arms form a bed or cushion beneath the tilted head.

Aurora's cradle is watched over by her nursemaid.

Attendant fairies bless the baby with gifts and dancing.

The Lilac Fairy graces the gathering with her elegance.

The Sleeping Beauty

AURORA'S BIRTHDAY PARTY

THE YEARS PASSED QUICKLY, and Aurora grew into a lovely, happy girl under her parents' watchful care. When Carabosse had uttered her wicked curse, the king issued a decree to protect Aurora. He banished every sharp object from the palace grounds, so no knife or needle could ever harm her.

One summer afternoon, all Aurora's friends gathered in the royal gardens to celebrate her sixteenth birthday. To their amazement, they noticed three old women knitting busily in the sun. "Grab them," the courtiers cried. "Stop that at once," the guards shouted. But when the queen took pity on the old women, the king forgave them.

"Where's my birthday girl?" the king laughed, and at last Aurora appeared, looking as radiant as a sunbeam. Four dashing princes had travelled from distant kingdoms in the hope of marrying her. Dazzled by her beauty and charm, they took turns flattering her and offered roses and compliments along with their hearts and kingdoms.

The courtiers carry garlands, ropes, or hoops, covered with flowers.

STEP: ATTITUDE
Aurora (Darcey Bussell) balances in an *attitude*. She stands on one leg and bends the other at a sharp angle directly behind her.

During Aurora's dance with her suitors, the Rose Adagio, she often returns to the attitude position.

The hopeful suitors cannot take their eyes off the graceful princess.

Aurora dances with all four of the visiting princes, twirling lightly from one to another.

Darting among them with a sweet smile, Aurora nearly collided with a shrivelled crone, who handed her a posy of fresh flowers concealing a shiny spindle. "Happy birthday, my dear," she croaked. Unaware of any danger, Aurora waved the posy gaily over her head and teasingly dodged everyone who tried to snatch it away.

Suddenly, the spindle's sharp tip pierced her finger. Crying out with surprise Aurora spun dizzily between her horrified guests and then crumpled to the ground. The crone tossed back her black hood and revealed her identity – it was Carabosse. With a triumphant cackle she disappeared in a flash of lightning.

As the queen bent over her child, the Lilac Fairy rose magically from the babble and confusion. "Carry Aurora into the palace," she said. "Remember, she is not dead. She is only sleeping." With her words, twisting vines began to wrap themselves around the marble columns of the palace. A veil of leaves drifted over its walls, and everyone inside fell asleep.

MARGOT FONTEYN (1919–91)
A great English ballerina who led the Royal Ballet for many years, Margot Fonteyn danced the role of Aurora with enchanting delicacy.

ROSE
Roses stand for love, and the pink rose is always linked with Aurora.

SPINDLE
A spindle is an old tool used for twisting yarn into thread on a spinning wheel.

When the king sees his daughter stretched out before him, he is sure she is dead.

Surprised by its sharp point, Aurora drops the spindle to the ground.

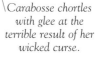

Carabosse chortles with glee at the terrible result of her wicked curse.

The Sleeping Beauty

A VISION APPEARS

♪ MUSICAL NOTE
Slow, mellow music is played to express the prince's sadness after he dismisses the court. The Lilac Fairy's lilting theme heralds her arrival.

COURTLY COSTUMES
Velvet skirts, tight-fitting jackets, and leather boots cause special problems for dancers. Thick fabrics slow their movements and boots are heavy and noisy.

A URORA SLEPT UNDISTURBED in the highest turret of the palace for one hundred years. Songbirds nested in the tangled briars and thick moss carpeted the stone stairs, and still no one came to break the spell.

Meanwhile, in a forest many miles away, a young prince, Florimund, went hunting one day with his friends. Everyone could see that the handsome prince was bored with the hunting and only joined the dancing so he would not offend his guests.

"Perhaps you would prefer a game of hide and seek?" his partner suggested cheerfully. But the prince wanted only to be left alone with his thoughts. "Let the royal hunt proceed without me," he finally commanded, dismissing his puzzled friends with a flourish.

Suddenly a voice echoed like rustling leaves in the stillness. "Why are you so unhappy?" asked the Lilac Fairy. Startled, Florimund bowed low before the shimmering creature who addressed him.

"I don't know why," he admitted sadly.

"I will show you something wonderful that will lift your spirits. Look," she urged.

Some of the courtiers ride off to hunt in another part of the forest.

The prince's friends leash the dogs while Florimund dances politely with a countess.

Florimund pays no attention to his elegant partner.

The prince raised his downcast eyes and saw a shimmering vision of Aurora, as light as a cloud.

"How beautiful she is," he exclaimed, and all at once the vision stood on the forest floor, surrounded by tiny fairies. The prince tiptoed nearer and stretched out his hand to touch her. Each time he came closer, the fairies flew between them. But at last, for a single instant, he held the vision of Aurora in his arms. The next instant, she was gone.

"Oh, no," he cried. "Please bring her back. I love her."

"If you love her," the Lilac Fairy answered, "you must go to her yourself and tell her so."

"I would go anywhere to find that princess again," Florimund declared bravely. So the Lilac Fairy led him across the fields and over the silvery seas to the palace where Aurora lay dreaming.

STEPS TELL THE STORY
Ballet steps are carefully organized, or choreographed, to be both dramatic and attractive. Here, the Lilac Fairy (Yuliana Lopatkina) separates Florimund and Aurora (Larissa Lezhnina) by standing between them.

MIME: SEE
The index fingers move down and away from the face from a position just below the eyes.

Florimund is captivated by Aurora's beauty.

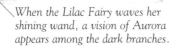

When the Lilac Fairy waves her shining wand, a vision of Aurora appears among the dark branches.

Their long voyage brings them to Aurora's palace.

Without hesitating, the prince boards the Lilac Fairy's boat.

The Sleeping Beauty

THE AWAKENING

♪ *MUSICAL NOTE*
The awakening scene opens with the themes for the Lilac Fairy, Carabosse, and the spindle intertwined. The music reaches its climax when a gong sounds as the prince kisses Aurora.

T HE SHADOWY PALACE WALLS towered over the Lilac Fairy's boat like a sleeping giant. Prince Florimund's heart pounded with excitement and fear as he pushed open the heavy, rusting gates and crossed the courtyard. Inside the cracked oaken door, the king's guards lay in snoring heaps.

The hallways were dark as caves. Not a single candle winked in the blackness, and Florimund

A cold wind has blown out every candle in the dusty room.

Silvery cobwebs cloud the air like fog.

Outside the palace grounds ordinary life goes on as usual.

The prince discovers Aurora, who is the vision he saw in the forest.

Florimund cuts his way towards the princess.

A dark tangle of ivy has wound itself across the wide staircase.

Even the dogs in the palace are sleeping soundly.

Ladies in waiting have also fallen under the spell.

could hear nothing but the creaking floorboards under his feet and the rattle of the wind in the tall towers. The Lilac Fairy glided along beside him, lighting his way with the glow of her magical presence.

Drawing his sword, Florimund bounded up the palace stairs, slashing at the knotted vines to clear a path. The dust stung his eyes and filled his throat. Spiders scurried over his hands, and mice skittered under his feet, but he climbed higher and higher, guided by the Lilac Fairy.

When he reached the topmost tower, he found Aurora stretched out on the silken bed, still as a corpse.

"She's dead," he groaned. "What shall I do?"

"She's not dead," promised the Lilac Fairy. "Think back. You must let her know you love her."

Florimund paused for a second, then leaned down and kissed Aurora tenderly. Her eyes fluttered open and, taking his hand, she sat up and thanked him with a smile as bright as a star.

Down in the throne room, the king and queen were brushing the cobwebs off each other's crowns. As they rose to their feet, Aurora burst into the room, pulling Florimund behind her.

"Here is the prince who broke the spell," she announced, "and he is the prince I choose for my husband."

Straight posture gives force to a gesture.

The legs can be in any position while the hands move.

MIME: LISTEN AND THINK
The boy mimes "listen" by tapping his middle fingers lightly to his ears. The girl mimes "think" by tapping her first two fingers twice against her temple. These mean the same whether a girl or boy performs them.

DRESSING THE STAGE
Léon Bakst (1866–1924) designed this costume for a Russian production of the ballet. It was worn by a page, who did not dance. His elaborate clothing was considered part of the stage decoration.

Florimund takes Aurora in his arms and vows never to let her go.

Aurora's love for the prince fills her with happiness and hope.

LIGHT AND DARK
Lighting helps create a specific atmosphere. Bright light floods the stage, as it does here, for happy occasions while pale light and deep shadows often surround sad or mysterious events.

The Sleeping Beauty

THE WEDDING

I N A TWINKLING, one hundred years of dust was swept away. The palace was polished until it shone, and bustling cooks baked dozens of delicious cakes while scurrying footmen filled all the rooms with fragrant wild roses and sprays of lilac.

On the day of Aurora's wedding to Florimund, sunlight as golden as honey flooded the banquet hall. Royal guests came from far and wide to wish the bride and groom long life and good fortune. Aurora herself invited her closest friends from childhood, who she introduced to her new husband one by one.

First the fluffy White Cat picked her way across the floor. With every step she glanced over her shoulder and winked at Puss in Boots, who bounded after her and scratched her back with his tickling paws.

BRILLIANT BLUEBIRD
This brief dance for the Bluebird (Tetsuya Kumakawa) is one of the most difficult male solos in ballet. It requires high leaps, quick turns, and fluttering beats where the feet crisscross many times in the air.

Guests from far and wide arrive for the wedding.

The hungry Wolf tries to catch Little Red Riding Hood and carry her away.

The Bluebird flies through his dizzying solo.

Princess Florine listens for the song of the glittering Bluebird, who will guide her away from her enchanter.

Four of the smallest pages carrying slim, gilded branches created a forest for Little Red Riding Hood. Licking his lips hungrily, the Wolf chased her through the trees. Then he pounced on her from behind, slung her over his shoulder, and loped off with a growl.

Next a pair of Bluebirds swooped and dipped above the guests' heads. One was really the enchanted Princess Florine, and the other was teaching her how to fly so she could escape from her enchanter. Their sparkling plumage reflected the sun as they soared in and out through the open windows.

Finally, Princess Aurora and Prince Florimund crowned the wedding celebration by declaring their love for each other.

"I love you," murmured Aurora. She was a little shy of speaking in front of so many people.

"I love you even more," answered Florimund.

The Lilac Fairy hovered over their heads, saying "Sharing your love and trust, you will surely live happily ever after."

STEP: FISH DIVE
In the final moments of Aurora and Florimund's duet (Ludmilla Semenyaka and Sergei Gorbachev), she dives towards him, curving her body like a fish. He supports her on one thigh and catches her legs under his arm.

Cooks from the royal kitchen baked a beautiful wedding cake.

Garlands of roses decorate the palace for this special day.

The king and queen are pleased at the happy match.

The Russian guests tumble into a lively folk dance.

When the fairy-tale creatures finish their entertainment, Aurora and Florimund proclaim their love for each other.

The White Cat and Puss in Boots perform a pas de chat (meaning "step of the cat").

FUR AND FEATHERS
When dancers portray animals, they often have to wear masks that cover their heads. The masks, although light in weight, are hot and stuffy to wear. Eyeholes must be carefully positioned so the dancers can see where they are going.

✻

FAIRY-TALE FACTS
The storybook characters at Aurora's wedding in the original production included Bluebeard, Goldilocks, Beauty and the Beast, Cinderella, and Tom Thumb. Some of them still appear today.

Giselle

The romantic story of *Giselle* was written by
Théophile Gautier and Vernoy de
St Georges. Jean Coralli and Jules Perrot
choreographed the ballet and
Adolphe Adam composed the music. The
first performance of *Giselle* was given at
the Opéra in Paris in 1841.

Giselle

IN THE VILLAGE

LONG AGO IN A VILLAGE far away, a pretty girl named Giselle lived with her mother in a thatched cottage. She was the happiest girl in the village, because she was madly in love with two things. One was dancing and the other was a boy, a newcomer to the village, named Loys. Giselle felt sure he loved her in return.

Her devotion to Loys greatly annoyed Hilarion, the local gamekeeper, because he loved Giselle too. However, neither of them knew that Loys was actually a count in disguise. He had noticed Giselle in the fields one day and come to the village to win her affection, hiding his true name and identity.

STEP: JETÉ
The French word *jeté* means "thrown". The dancer throws one leg up and away from the body. The body is thrown too, from one foot to the other. Giselle (Margarita Kullik) performs big (*grands*) *jetés*, like this one, as well as small (*petits*) *jetés*.

The dancer's arms should make a frame for the face without covering it.

MIME: DANCE
With the arms raised over the head, the dancer's hands circle each other smoothly, moving from soft, flexible wrists.

Loys hides his sword and velvet cloak from the villagers.

Berthe worries that her daughter, Giselle, will exhaust herself.

Daisies grow wild around the cottage.

One morning he coaxed her away from her chores and flattered her until she blushed pink.

"Do you really love me?" she asked. "Honestly?"

"Of course I do. You have my promise," he answered.

"Catch me if you can," giggled Giselle, dodging his embrace playfully, but Loys caught up with her. Tucking her arm through his, he led her and all her friends into a merry dance.

Hilarion could not bear to watch. "What about me?" he protested.

Knowing her response would hurt his feelings, Giselle said nothing, but her glowing eyes spoke for her. She would gladly have danced with Loys forever.

She was disappointed when her mother came bustling into the clearing and took charge. "That is enough dancing for one morning," she scolded. "You will wear yourself out."

As Giselle threw Loys a kiss and skipped indoors, Hilarion suddenly had an idea. When he was quite alone, he drew his dagger, picked the lock on Loys' cottage and sneaked inside.

HE LOVES ME, HE LOVES ME NOT
Giselle (Leanne Benjamin) pulls the petals off a daisy, one by one. Each petal speaks about a lover's feelings. The first says his love is true, the next denies it. She hopes the last petal will tell her that Loys (Bruce Sansom) sincerely loves her.

The nobles who live in the distant castle seldom visit the vineyards.

Loys' cottage is so simple that no-one suspects his real identity.

Ignoring her mother's advice, Giselle dances with Loys as much as she can.

Hilarion breaks into Loys' cottage, to satisfy his curiosity about the stranger.

Charmed by Giselle's gaiety, Loys is happy to remain in disguise.

LOVE OF DANCE
The passion that Giselle (Fiona Chadwick) feels for dancing runs through the entire ballet and causes all the important events.

Giselle

THE BETRAYAL

♪ *MUSICAL NOTE*
The music in the mad scene contains parts of the daisy theme and of the melody marking Giselle's love for Loys. The short phrases echo her broken thoughts.

ALICIA MARKOVA
(*BORN 1910*)
The first British ballerina to take the role of Giselle was Alicia Markova. She became a professional dancer at the age of 14, and later co-founded the company now called English National Ballet.

HILARION EMERGED FROM Loys' cottage, frowning and confused. He was holding a long velvet cloak and a gleaming silver sword. What did they mean?

Before he could decide, a trumpet flourish forced him into hiding. The duke and the elegant countess, Bathilde, swept into the clearing, with a splendid party of noblemen and ladies close behind.

Everyone came running to peer at the courtly nobles. Awed by their embroidered clothes and golden jewels, Giselle and her mother curtsied low and offered the visitors a refreshing drink.

"Tell me, dear" said Bathilde, "what do you do all day?"

"I love to dance," Giselle admitted, skipping shyly through a few steps.

Hot and tired after his long walk, the Duke relaxes in the shade.

The visitors enjoy the cool drinks Giselle and her mother have provided.

Bathilde is charmed by Giselle's admiration.

Giselle poses for her friends as they crown her Queen of the Vineyards.

Giselle has never seen such a splendid gown.

"Are you in love too?" asked Bathilde.

"Yes," smiled Giselle, but when she could not spot Loys among her friends, she entertained Bathilde by herself, leaping and spinning gaily.

Praising her graceful performance, the guests withdrew for a rest. Just then Loys returned to the clearing, and as Giselle began to describe her encounter, Hilarion thrust Loys' sword between them.

"Ask Loys about this," he demanded. "He is not a peasant at all."

"I do not believe you," said Giselle, shaking her head.

"Look at the crest," Hilarion insisted. He held the sword beside a hunting horn left hanging on a nail, and their crests matched perfectly. Then he blew the horn, and the nobles answered its call at once.

"Count Albrecht," exclaimed Bathilde. "What are you doing here?"

Loys tried to pretend his disguise was a joke, but Giselle understood the truth. "Leave him alone," she cried, "he is going to marry me."

"No," Bathilde retorted, "he is going to marry me."

Giselle's mind suddenly snapped. Heartbroken and mad with grief, she lurched from Loys to Hilarion to her mother, recognizing no-one. Finally, with a great gasp, she collapsed and died.

STEP: *DÉVELOPPÉ*
Giselle (Yulia Makhalina) performs this movement when dancing with her friends. The name of the step means "develop", or "unfold". One leg gradually unfolds, to the front, side, or back, as it rises into the air. At its highest point, the leg is fully stretched.

Deeply ashamed, Loys turns his face away as Hilarion reveals his secret to Giselle.

Giselle's madness horrifies her friends, but they cannot calm her.

Blinded by her tears, the crazed girl stumbles when she tries to dance.

In her madness, Giselle believes the sword is a wriggling snake.

Bathilde's gift to Giselle lies on the ground.

RUINED DREAMS
Giselle's mad scene is a sad dance of gestures and expressions rather than steps. Dramatic dancers (Fiona Tomkin and Steven Heathcote) act with their bodies and faces.

Giselle

THE REALM OF THE WILIS

♪ *MUSICAL NOTE*
In near silence, the midnight chime of the town clock rings out clearly. Then deep rising cello notes mirror the approach of the Wilis through the dark forest.

CARLOTTA GRISI (1819–99)
Grisi was the first person to dance the role of Giselle, which was specially created for her. She was ideal for the part because her lightness and delicacy convinced the audience that she was a spirit.

LILY

ROSEMARY

FLOWER SYMBOLS
The lily is associated with death, so it is bad luck to include it in a dancer's bouquet. Rosemary was once carried at weddings and funerals because it stands for remembrance.

❋

SUPERNATURAL POWER
The dancer portraying Giselle often rises from the grave draped in a wedding veil. A fine, invisible wire makes it disappear as if by magic.

SEVERAL NIGHTS LATER, Hilarion ventured into the woods to visit Giselle's grave. Dampness chilled him to the bone, and ghostly creatures flitted past him like huge moths. Terrified, he ran deeper into the forest to avoid them.

As midnight struck, a regal figure emerged from the shimmering shadows. Myrtha, Queen of the Wilis, circled her dark, cold realm and then, whisking her wand overhead, summoned her subjects from all over the world. The Wilis instantly surrounded her in a cloud of wings and gossamer gowns. They were

Giselle bows humbly to her haughty queen.

Myrtha, Queen of the Wilis, welcomes Giselle to the spirit world.

the spirits of girls who had died before their weddings, and they all loved to dance. So every night they rose eagerly from their graves, hoping to find a partner who would dance with them until dawn.

Veiled and pale as moonlight, Giselle stepped suddenly from their midst and whirled into her first dance with her new sisters. When the crackle of twigs announced a visitor, they darted into the shadows. Albrecht knelt beside Giselle's grave and covered it with lilies and tears, knowing his lies had destroyed her.

"Now I will never see her again," he wept, yet there she was, right beside him, like a statue carved out of flowing mist. Torn between joy and fear, he tried to embrace her, but his hands grabbed empty air. As she drifted through the trees, Albrecht ran after her with outstretched arms. "Wait," he called, "please forgive me. I do love you."

The forest closed around them, but it could not protect Hilarion, who had stumbled among the Wilis. Obeying Myrtha's command he danced with every Wili until exhaustion overcame him. Too dizzy to see, Hilarion reached for his next partner and plunged to his death in the icy pond.

SURE AND STEADY
Through constant practice, dancers learn to help each other in different ways. Supporting his partner with his back, Julio Arozarena helps Nadia Dimitrova create the illusion that Giselle is weightless.

ROMANTIC BALLET
Between 1830 and 1870, many ballets told stories of men who fell in love with elusive spirits. Giselle exists in both the real world and as a fantasy in Albrecht's dreams.

As Myrtha's loyal handmaidens, the Wilis carry out her orders.

Like a vision, Giselle is always just out of Albrecht's reach.

Cold, pale, and silent, the Wilis gather at midnight to seek a partner for their frenzied dance. No man can hide from them.

Giselle throws flowers to the astonished Albrecht.

Giselle
THE TRIUMPH OF LOVE

♪ *MUSICAL NOTE*
The composer chose the viola, which seldom carries the melody, for Giselle's mournful solo. The sad, fragile sound of harps supports a single flute as Giselle fades into the pale sunlight and disappears into her grave for the last time.

FANTASTIC PHANTOMS
An old legend describes the Wilis as angry creatures. As young girls, they were all abandoned by the men who had promised to marry them. In death they become stern spirits who demand their revenge each night (Benazir Hussein as Myrtha, above).

POINTE SHOE
During the Romantic era, ballet shoes changed so a dancer could stand on her toes. Silk slippers were padded with cotton wool and, years later, stiffened with glue to support the feet.

BEFORE THE WATERS CLOSED over Hilarion's head, the Wilis found their next partner. Sensing the danger all around him, Albrecht approached Myrtha with caution and respect. As she began to speak, Giselle flew past him like thistledown in the wind and placed herself between him and her fierce queen.

Her body told Albrecht what he must do. "Stand by the cross on my grave," it seemed to say. "You will be safe there." With a gentle nod, she guided him out of Myrtha's reach.

The Wilis surround Albrecht, who takes refuge behind Giselle.

Myrtha carries a sprig of rosemary.

The queen did not expect such resistance, but her power could not touch Albrecht as long as the cross and Giselle's love protected him. She then ordered Giselle to dance alone, luring her away from Albrecht. Giselle could not refuse.

Albrecht realized he was in danger, but his love for Giselle drew him to her side. Folding his arms gently around her, he danced with her all night, and as long as they remained together, nothing could harm him.

The moon sailed across the black sky during their silent dance and starlight frosted the forest floor. Albrecht grew more tired and frightened as each hour passed. "Please let me go," he begged Myrtha and the Wilis, but they all turned their backs.

Giselle never abandoned him. Every time he stumbled, she danced in his place, giving him time to recover his strength again. All at once, sunlight soft as gold dust powdered the treetops. The night was over, and Giselle's love had kept Albrecht alive. The Wilis and Giselle melted away like the morning mist. Nothing remained of her except in Albrecht's memory and in his hands, where she left a rosebud as a farewell kiss.

STEP: CABRIOLE
In this big jump, one leg kicks quickly to the side, front, or back. The dancer leaves the ground when he lifts his other leg to meet the first in mid-air. Albrecht (Konstantin Zaklinsky) is leaping for his life.

✱

A MOMENT'S REST
After many jumps and turns, Albrecht finishes his difficult solo lying down. He can catch his breath while the audience applauds.

MIME: DIE
The arms open to the side, where the hands form tight fists. Then the arms curve closed in front of the body. As the wrists cross, the arms drop with a swift jerk.

The forceful gesture seems to break life in two.

Giselle touches Albrecht for the last time before she returns to her grave.

Giselle leaves Albrecht a wild rosebud as a keepsake.

Thanks to Giselle, Albrecht has survived, but he will never see her again.

Coppélia

The tale of *Coppélia* was written by Charles Nuitter and Arthur Saint-Léon, from a story by E. T. A. Hoffmann. The comic ballet was choreographed by Saint-Léon; Léo Delibes composed the music. The first performance took place at the Opéra in Paris in 1870. Most productions today are based on the version choreographed by Marius Petipa in 1884 and later revised by Enrico Cecchetti.

Coppélia

THE LOVERS QUARREL

♪ MUSICAL NOTE
During a walking trip in Hungary, the composer, Léo Delibes, made notes on the music of the local folk dances. In the ballet, he used the tunes and rhythms he had heard.

I N A COUNTRY VILLAGE, near the top of a distant mountain, lived an old inventor named Dr Coppélius and his daughter, Coppélia. Every day Coppélia sat on her balcony reading a book, but she never moved or said a word. Even Swanilda, the friendliest girl in the village, could not make her speak.

One morning, Swanilda skipped into the square, looking for her boyfriend, Franz. She was amazed to find him grinning up at Coppélia and throwing her kisses like confetti.

"Flirts make terrible husbands," Swanilda blurted out, startling Franz with her sharp words. Before he could explain himself, their friends crowded around them, chattering about the new bell.

"It will ring tomorrow for all new brides," the burgomaster told Swanilda. "Will you be one of them?"

WHISPERING WHEAT
Following an old custom, Swanilda (Lis Jeppesen) shakes an ear of wheat and listens closely. It will murmur her lover's name if he is true, but it remains sadly silent.

MIME: FLIRT
The dancer kisses the back of his own hands, one right after the other.

QUICK CHANGE
Dancers must learn how to alter their manner and expressions for different ballets. Here, Fernando Bujones plays Franz, a jaunty yokel. He might appear as a noble prince a few days later.

Swanilda is annoyed by Franz's behaviour.

Franz thinks he is alone when he tries to coax a smile from Coppélia.

Unable to hide her tears, Swanilda shook her head sadly and dashed away, leaving Franz to shrug his shoulders in innocent confusion.

That evening, when Dr Coppélius left his mysterious tinkering and scurried outside for a stroll, several boys jumped from the shadows to frighten him, just for fun. The old man whacked them with his cane and finally chased them off. Hearing the commotion Swanilda and her friends rushed into the square, but by then everyone had disappeared.

Something bright in the dust caught Swanilda's eye. It was Dr Coppélius' house key, which he had dropped in the scuffle.

"What luck," she cried. "Now we can meet Coppélia face to face."

"Oh, no," wailed the girls, hanging back. "Go in there? By ourselves? Absolutely not!"

"Then I will go alone," Swanilda laughed.

Shamed by her courage, Swanilda's friends swallowed their fear and tiptoed after her. Just as they vanished, Franz sneaked into the moonlit square carrying a ladder. He had made his own plans, and was going to visit Coppélia too.

FOLK DANCING
Coppélia brought the czardas, a lively Hungarian folk dance, to European ballet for the first time. Later, choreographers introduced many other national and traditional dances to the stage.

The girls slip into Dr Coppélius' house.

Franz nears the house just as the girls disappear inside.

The villagers stamp and whirl in the bright sun.

Franz ignores Swanilda's angry outburst.

Coppélia

In the workshop

SAUCY SOUBRETTE
Swanilda (Margaret Tracey) is the ideal role for a *soubrette* – a dancer with high spirits, bubbly charm, and a lively talent for comic acting.

Under his make-up, the dancer playing Dr. Coppélius could be any age at all.

CHARACTER MAKE-UP
Dancers can change their looks with false eyebrows and hair, putty noses, and rubber cheeks. Greasepaint is applied to alter the colour of their skin and create age lines and deep shadows.

TOO FRIGHTENED EVEN TO WHISPER, the girls crept nervously into Dr Coppélius' workshop. They saw folded arms, glassy eyes, and crumpled bodies, all as still as stones. Pulling back a dusty curtain, Swanilda discovered Coppélia, sitting in her usual chair, reading her usual book.

"Hello," she said politely, but of course she got no answer.

She moved closer. "Has the cat got your tongue?" she asked. Again, no answer. So she reached out and tugged Coppélia's skirt. Still nothing happened.

Inching even closer Swanilda stared straight into her rival's face and dissolved into giggles. "She will never answer us," she announced to her quaking friends, "because she is a doll! They are all dolls!"

Whooping with delight, the girls wound up the toys and danced among them, causing havoc in the workshop.

Coppélia does not look at Swanilda or move a muscle.

Swanilda pulls back the curtain and finds her rival.

They made so much noise that Dr Coppélius appeared in their midst without being noticed.

"Get out, all of you," he bellowed, swinging his cane at their legs as they sprinted away. Swanilda knew she could not escape, so when his back was turned she ducked behind Coppélia's curtain.

Alone at last, Dr Coppélius was still patting the dolls into place when Franz slipped into the workshop from the balcony and began to explore. The old man could hardly believe it. "Why am I cursed with so much trouble?" he wondered, but now he was ready for intruders.

"What do you want?" he barked, seizing Franz by the arm.

"I… I want to marry your daughter," Franz spluttered.

Dr Coppélius smiled warmly but his eyes were cold as ice. A brilliant idea flared in his mind like a candle.

"Have a drink with me," he murmured, "and then we will discuss it like friends." He tugged Franz into a chair and filled his glass again and again, first mixing the wine with a magic potion. When Franz fell asleep, Dr Coppélius rolled up his sleeves and went to work.

HUMAN DOLLS
To be convincing as dolls, dancers must have the discipline to stand still for long periods of time without drawing attention to themselves. Their movement should be a complete surprise to the audience.

19TH-CENTURY FRENCH MECHANICAL DOLL

MECHANICAL DOLLS
Coppélia is one of the first ballets about dolls that come to life. Its subtitle, "The Girl with the Enamel Eyes", describes both the heroine, Swanilda, and the doll who is her rival.

✱

DANCING DOLLS
In another ballet, *Petrouchka*, all the leading characters are dolls: Petrouchka the clown, the ballerina he loves, and the fierce Moor who kills him.

The figures dangling from the rafters sway gently in the dark.

Spanish doll

Dr Coppélius chases his visitors away.

Scottish doll

Coppélia

WISHES COME TRUE

P USHING COPPÉLIA'S CHAIR into the centre of the room, Dr Coppélius gazed at her proudly. She was the most beautiful doll he had ever made, and now he was going to bring her to life.

He consulted the diagrams in his magic books and mumbled some ancient spells. Then he drew the energy from Franz's eyes, muscles, and bones, and thrust it towards Coppélia. First her eyes blinked. Then her shoulders wiggled. After that, she stood up and took a few stiff steps.

Dr Coppélius fell back in amazement, watching his doll move and turn by herself, and his hopes rose even higher. Concentrating with all his might, he dragged his hands across Franz's chest, absorbing the beat of his heart and guiding it into Coppélia.

A gentle smile curved her lips and she started to breathe. Dr Coppélius trembled with joy as he laid his ear against her chest and listened to her heartbeat.

"Of course my heart is beating," Swanilda was

MUSICAL NOTE
A single rich horn note sounds when Dr Coppélius first injects energy into Swanilda. The cello and double-bass players pluck their strings, or play them *pizzicato*, to accentuate each abrupt movement as she makes it.

DANCING WITHOUT STEPS
Mime roles require a mix of acting and natural gestures. Dr Coppélius (Gideon Louw) moves naturally, without using ballet positions, even when he is partnering Swanilda (Hiroko Sakakibara).

ALEXANDRA DANILOVA AS SWANILDA IN 1949.

ALEXANDRA DANILOVA
(BORN 1903)
Danilova first danced in *Coppélia* as a student in St Petersburg, Russia. She became a sparkling Swanilda and then a respected teacher.

Keeping her arms and legs rigid, Swanilda stares straight ahead.

Dr Coppélius cannot believe his eyes when the doll starts to move.

The book of magic spells

thinking. "I am a real live person. Any fool could see that."

Dr Coppélius was not a fool, but his love for his creation blinded him to the truth. He did not realize Swanilda had put on the doll's dress and was pretending to be Coppélia. The faster she danced the happier he became.

Swanilda grew tired of her disguise when she noticed Franz, snoring at the table. While she tried to wake him, she set all the dolls in motion, hoping her mischief would distract Dr Coppélius.

"Be a good girl, please," the old man protested, stumbling after her to undo the damage, but Swanilda ignored him. Yanking Franz to his feet she shoved him towards the door, and they ran into the night together.

Left alone, poor Dr Coppélius collapsed in despair. Beside him flopped the twisted body of his dear Coppélia, who had never really come to life at all.

A FAN TO HAND
The props, or properties, that dancers use on stage must be in exactly the right place at the right time. Swanilda (Miranda Coney) dances a Spanish fandango because Dr Coppélius gives her a fan. The fan must always be ready for him in the hands of the Spanish doll.

Dr Coppélius fears that Coppélia will never be as good as new.

The fingers remain soft and the palms turned down.

Swanilda dances a jig, wearing the Scottish doll's tartan sash.

Overcome by the drugged wine, Franz sees and hears nothing.

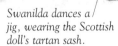

Dr Coppélius' work trunk overflows with hats, buttons, and ribbons.

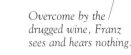

MIME: NO
The hands cross at the wrist, swing apart and then cross again. Finally they open firmly as if brushing away any argument. The gesture can be forceful or gentle.

Coppélia
A DAY TO CELEBRATE

♪ MUSICAL NOTE
The composer planned the final act as a Festival of Bells. He wrote music for the different occasions when the new bell would ring – for Dawn, Prayer, Work, War, Marriage, and the Hours of the Day.

A CHOICE OF ENDINGS
The final scene of the original *Coppélia* was dropped two years after the first performance, and many endings have replaced it. A grumpy Dr Coppélius often leaves the scene to return to work, but sometimes he cheers up and joins the celebration.

DISGUISING THE TRUTH
When this ballet was first created, male dancers were so unpopular they were used on stage only to carry women. For many years, Franz (played here by David McAllister) was danced by a woman *en travesti*, disguised as a man.

BRIGHT AND EARLY THE NEXT MORNING, all the villagers assembled on the rolling lawn of the manor house. The lord of the manor had promised the town a new bell and invited everyone to celebrate its arrival from the foundry.

Trellises of flowers caught the sunlight in a net of many colours, and crisp banners flapped in the breeze. All the young couples received a blessing and a small dowry from the generous lord.

With their arms entwined, Swanilda and Franz led the parade of radiant brides and handsome grooms. Just as the burgomaster was thanking the local lord for the shiny new bell, a gloomy shadow fell across the lawn.

Dr Coppélius had wrapped Coppélia in a blanket and brought her along from the workshop. He was furious. "I want an

The villagers bring the new bell to church.

Coppélia hangs limply in her maker's arms.

Dr Coppélius is already imagining new ways to bring his dolls to life.

A bag of gold helps lift Dr Coppélius' spirits.

explanation," he grumbled, pointing to the ruined doll. "I want an apology. I must be paid for the damage. I demand justice."

Swanilda and Franz begged him to forgive them for their prank. "Please take my dowry," said Swanilda. "It is not much, but maybe it will be enough to repay you for the trouble we caused. We never meant to harm you with our tricks."

She smiled so sweetly and spoke so sincerely that Dr Coppélius forgave her at once, and when the burgomaster handed him a bag of gold coins, his anger evaporated. Muttering gruff good wishes to Swanilda and all the pretty brides, he trotted happily back to his workshop and his faithful dolls.

Franz hugged Swanilda as hard as he could, and she hugged him back. "No more dolls for me," he promised. "A real girl is more lively than a mechanical one and more fun too. I gladly give you my heart, Swanilda."

"Good," she said, with a wink to her girlfriends, "I am delighted to accept it."

NOTATION TO THE RESCUE
Writing down, or notating, steps preserves movement that might be forgotten. The original steps for *Coppélia* were never notated, so Margaret Tracey and Damian Woetzel perform new ones created in 1974.

Franz knows he has chosen the right girl.

The new brides and grooms celebrate their weddings.

Swanilda feels content at last, certain that Franz will be a faithful husband.

AN OVERNIGHT STAR
The search for the perfect Swanilda lasted for three years. When Guiseppina Bozzacchi won the part in 1869, she was only 16 and had never danced in public.

Swan Lake

The dramatic ballet *Swan Lake*, for which
Tchaikovsky composed the music, failed
when it was first staged in Moscow in 1877.
Lev Ivanov and Marius Petipa then
choreographed a new version. Their
Swan Lake was first performed in 1895 at the
Maryinsky Theatre in St Petersburg.

♪ MUSICAL NOTE
At the end of this scene, the composer introduces the ballet's only musical theme, the swan theme. The oboe carries the mournful melody, which is heard many times throughout the ballet.

A ROYAL ROLE
In the ballet, the queen must appear gracious and dignified. The role is usually played by a mature and experienced dancer, who can convey authority with firm conviction.

MIME: MARRY
To mime the word "marry", the dancer extends both hands in front of the body and points to the base of the left ring finger with the index finger of the right hand.

Swan Lake

THE PRINCE COMES OF AGE

HIGH IN THE MOUNTAINS of a distant land, far above the villages and farms, Prince Siegfried and his mother, the queen, lived quietly in a great stone castle. Every year, on the afternoon of the prince's birthday, they invited the local farmers and villagers and all the prince's friends from the surrounding estates to a big party.

When Siegfried reached the age of manhood, his birthday celebration was livelier than ever and he seemed entirely happy. He laughed at his friends' jokes

Sentries watch the party from a castle tower.

Siegfried welcomes his friends to a day of celebration.

Villagers raise their glasses in a toast to the prince.

Courtiers waltz gaily beneath the castle's stone battlements.

and graciously accepted the good wishes of the high-spirited villagers.

Then his friend Benno pointed towards the castle. "Here comes your mother," he whispered. "Let me take your wine glass, before she sees it." Siegfried welcomed the queen warmly, and his eyes lit up when she presented him with a gleaming crossbow for a birthday present.

As he began to thank her, she interrupted him briskly. "We have serious matters to discuss," she said. "Now that you are old enough to succeed me on the throne, it is time for you to get married."

"But I am not in love," Siegfried protested with a grin.

"That is not important," the queen continued. "I have invited all the eligible young ladies in the land to the ball tomorrow night. Before the evening ends, you must choose your bride."

Siegfried was thunderstruck, but he bowed obediently and hid his distress until she was out of sight.

"Cheer up," said Benno. "You can still enjoy yourself today." As he spoke, a flock of swans flew across the evening sky. "Why not try your new crossbow?" Benno suggested. The powerful, wild birds captured Siegfried's attention and raised his spirits.

"A hunt is a wonderful idea," he agreed. Seizing his crossbow, he led his friends into the deepening darkness.

LIFTING AND LEAPING
Holding a large or heavy object makes dancing more difficult than usual. The crossbow's weight and size force Siegfried (Jeremy Collins) to adjust his balance and lower his jumps.

The swans pass silently overhead.

Siegfried admires the crossbow the queen has given him.

The queen tells her son he must think seriously about marriage.

♪ MUSICAL NOTE
The composer wrote bouncy, hopping rhythms for the oboes and bassoons to accompany the short, quick dance of the four little cygnets.

STEP: ARABESQUE
To perform an *arabesque*, the dancer balances on one leg, stretching her other leg straight out behind her. In this position, Odette (Sylvie Guillem) resembles a swan in flight.

Swan Lake

BESIDE THE LAKE

S IEGFRIED AND HIS FRIENDS followed the ancient, winding paths into the darkest part of the forest. When they reached the silvery lake and spied the wild swans gliding on the surface, Siegfried raised his crossbow and took aim.

At that moment, the nearest swan left the water in a flurry of beating wings and became a beautiful woman, who arched her neck proudly and preened in the moonlight. She drew back in alarm when she saw Siegfried, but he stood perfectly still so he would not frighten her.

"Who are you?" he asked in amazement.

"I am Odette, Queen of the Swans," she answered. "An evil sorcerer named Rothbart has cast a spell on me and all

Safe in Siegfried's arms, Odette feels sure she can trust him.

The swans guard Odette from Rothbart's anger.

✳

SWANS WITHOUT A STORY
At one time, ballet companies often performed the lakeside scene without the rest of the ballet. They slipped it in between other short works to create a varied programme.

these swans. We can return to human form only between midnight and dawn. I beg you not to shoot us."

"I would not harm you," Siegfried said gently. "How can I help you?"

"Rothbart's wicked spell will last forever," Odette explained, "unless someone falls in love with me, promises to marry me, and swears he will never love anyone else."

Fascinated by her sad tale, Siegfried wrapped his arms protectively around her, and tenderness filled his heart. "I love you," he declared, "and I will always be faithful." Their love grew stronger as the hours passed, and the swan maidens shared their happiness.

Rothbart remained hidden in the shadows, gloating over the plight of his innocent subjects. When dawn broke, he rose up over them, with his dark wings spread, and ordered them back to the lake. Odette tried frantically to resist, but Rothbart's magic dragged her out of Siegfried's arms. In another instant she was gone, and the stunned prince was alone, gazing helplessly into the sky as the swans flew away.

PAS DE DEUX
To be comfortable and beautiful in a *pas de deux* (dance for two), the dancers' bodies must fit neatly together (Elizabeth Loscavio and Anthony Randazzo). If the woman is taller or heavier than her partner, he cannot support or lift her.

ROTHBART THE EVIL SORCERER
The character of Rothbart (Dorio Perez) never changes, but his costume is always different. In some versions of the ballet, he looks like an owl or a vulture, in others he appears as a man.

Rothbart uses his evil power to separate Odette and Siegfried.

Odette bids farewell to her new love with a gentle kiss.

Siegfried cannot prevent Odette from leaving.

THE CYGNETS
The French word for "little swans" is also the title of this famous dance. Four of the smallest dancers perform exactly the same steps at the same time, keeping their hands linked until the last moment.

Swan Lake

AT THE BALL

♪ *MUSICAL NOTE*
Repeated trumpet fanfares help set the scene and move the action along. They announce the arrival of the entertainers and the princesses, as well as the unexpected guests – Odile and Rothbart.

DIVERTISSEMENT
This French word, which means "diversion", refers to the colourful dances that show off the performers without advancing the story. Here they include a Neapolitan dance (shown above), a Spanish bolero, and a Polish mazurka.

T HE FOLLOWING NIGHT, the palace was ablaze with candles and crammed with guests for Siegfried's birthday ball. Entertainers from Spain, Hungary, Poland, and Italy wore spangled robes that shimmered in the firelight, and the air smelled of perfume.

Knowing they were on display, the princesses curtsied low before Siegfried and struggled to attract his interest. They admired his palace and praised the visiting performers, but he scarcely bothered to respond. Instead he escorted them through the dances and then simply walked away. He could think of nothing but his beloved Odette.

"Will you chose a bride from these lovely girls?" the queen finally demanded.

"No, I will not," said Siegfried, stubbornly defying his mother's wishes. Before she had time to apologize to the

Odette hopes that Siegfried remembers his promise.

Siegfried holds Odile tightly, convinced she is the woman he met by the lake.

Odile captivates Siegfried with her beauty.

The princesses understand that Siegfried will never marry any of them.

embarrassed princesses a crack of thunder shook the palace walls, and two mysterious guests appeared from nowhere. One was Rothbart, transformed into a tall, stately count. The other, his daughter, Odile, had been transformed too, so that she looked like Odette.

Convinced that Odette had come to join him, Siegfried embraced Odile happily and whirled her into a rapturous dance. Odile bewitched him with her glittering beauty, so he never noticed the real Odette fluttering anxiously at the window to remind him of his promise.

At last, breathless with excitement, he announced to the astonished court that he would marry Odile. "Are you certain you love her?" murmured Rothbart. "Do you swear it?"

Siegfried raised his arm and swore his love, and the count burst into mocking laughter. "You have betrayed Odette," he cried, "and now she is mine forever." He tossed his cloak around Odile, and they vanished.

At once Siegfried realized that he had been tricked. Without a word, he raced out of the ballroom, desperate to find Odette and right the terrible wrong he had committed.

A FLASH OF DANGER
The same steps constantly reappear in ballets. The character performing them, and the dramatic situation, changes the effect of the step. In this *arabesque*, Odile (Daria Klimentova) makes her arms and legs look sharp and dangerous.

Court musicians play to announce the royal guests.

Odile tricks Siegfried into a proposal of marriage.

No-one recognizes Rothbart, the evil sorcerer.

Siegfried can hardly wait to claim his bride.

IN THE SPOTLIGHT
This solo gives Siegfried (Laurent Hilaire) a chance to display difficult steps. The original steps have been lost, so each dancer replaces them with the most dazzling turns and leaps he can perform.

Swan Lake

THE LOVERS ARE UNITED

♪ MUSICAL NOTE
To evoke the sadness of the swans, Tchaikovsky composed a group dance with slow, heavy rhythms and a plaintive melody. When the swan theme returns, it echoes Odette's agitation.

ANNA PAVLOVA (1881–1931)
A Russian ballerina of fragile charm and grace, Anna Pavlova toured the world with her own company for more than 20 years. In 1907 Michel Fokine created a dramatic solo, *The Dying Swan* (*Le Cygne*), for her. It became her signature role.

CORPS DE BALLET
This French term means "body of the ballet". The dancers who form this group enliven the action, frame the leading artists; and enhance the atmosphere of each scene. The corps members are usually a company's youngest, least experienced dancers.

WHEN ODETTE RETURNED to the forest alone, the swans saw glistening tears on her cheeks. "I have failed you," she told them. "Siegfried has broken his promise and betrayed me. Now we have little hope of escaping from Rothbart's spell."

The swans flocked around to console her, but her sorrow increased as the night wore on and Siegfried did not appear. "Be patient," the swans urged. "He will come to you as soon as he recognizes his mistake."

Odette was in despair. "I cannot live like this forever," she sobbed. "I would rather die."

Suddenly a violent storm whipped across the lake, blowing her fearful words away.

As the swans

Happy to be together again, Odette and Siegfried dance before the dawn breaks.

huddled together in the wind, trying to calm Odette, Siegfried dashed into their midst and threw himself at her feet.

"Please forgive me," he said. "I never forgot you and I never loved anyone else. Rothbart tricked me."

Odette embraced him joyfully and forgave him with all her heart. In the peaceful hush after the storm, the lovers agreed never to part again.

"You are still mine," roared Rothbart, swooping down on them from the darkness, "and I will not release you." He snatched Odette from Siegfried's grasp and attacked the prince directly. Siegfried fought him fiercely, shielding Odette as he battled for her freedom.

When Rothbart stumbled and fell, Odette seized her chance. Kissing Siegfried one last time, she climbed the rocks and threw herself into the lake, choosing death over everlasting enchantment. Siegfried could not bear to lose her a second time. With a mighty effort, he flung Rothbart aside and hurled himself into the lake after Odette.

At last they were united, and the overwhelming power of their love defeated Rothbart and destroyed his magic.

Shrieking hideously, he collapsed in a heap of feathers as the swan maidens emerged from their spell into the new day.

PORT DE BRAS
This French phrase means "the carriage of the arms". It stands for the graceful arrangement of the arms in relation to the body and the character. In the role of Odette, Stephanie Dabney uses her arms like wings.

Rothbart's evil power begins to fade.

Odette's love for Siegfried overcomes her fear of Rothbart.

Siegfried tries to protect Odette from Rothbart's fury.

The Nutcracker

The fantastic ballet of *The Nutcracker* was choreographed by Lev Ivanov to music composed by Tchaikovsky. Marius Petipa wrote the story, which he based on a German tale by E. T. A. Hoffmann. The first performance of this ballet took place at the Maryinsky Theatre in St Petersburg in 1892.

The Nutcracker

CHRISTMAS EVE

O NE FROSTY CHRISTMAS EVE many years ago, a family by the name of Stahlbaum, gave a big, festive party. Clara and her little brother Fritz were so excited they could hardly wait for it to begin. When the guests finally arrived, all the children raced into the drawing room ahead of their parents to see the candlelit tree and to examine the shiny packages nestled beneath its branches.

"Your godfather is here," called Clara's mother over the hubbub of chattering and laughter. Clara ran over to greet Herr Drosselmeyer. Although he was old and quite strange, she liked him very much.

"This is my nephew," Drosselmeyer announced, nudging the boy forward to shake Clara's hand. "I have also

♪ MUSICAL NOTE
The composer chose toy instruments, including a trumpet, miniature drum, and tiny cymbals, to accompany the children's excitement and noisy games in the opening scene. A rattle makes the dry sound of the nutcracker's jaws.

CHILDREN ON STAGE
The children who dance in this ballet often play several parts. At the start, as ordinary children, they must seem natural and relaxed. Later, they might appear again as mice, soldiers, or sweets.

Children search for small gifts among the tree branches.

A box of toy soldiers stands at the foot of the Christmas tree.

The performing dolls are named Harlequin and Columbine.

Clara and Drosselmeyer's nephew quickly become friends.

brought your Christmas presents." Turning the hidden keys, he set three glittering dolls twirling, just like real people. Eyes wide with amazement, the children fell silent to watch them dance before the precious toys were whisked away for safe-keeping.

"I have a special gift for a special girl," said Drosselmeyer. He drew a painted wooden soldier out of his deep pocket and showed Clara how to crack nuts between its hinged jaws. "What a wonderful nutcracker," Clara exclaimed. "Thank you. This is the best present of all."

"Give it to me," shouted Fritz, jealously pushing the girls aside. As he grabbed the nutcracker from Clara, it slipped through his fingers and broke on the floor.

Before Clara could cry, Drosselmeyer bandaged the nutcracker's head with his handkerchief. "He will be fine by morning," he promised Clara, who was tucking the wounded toy into one of her doll's beds. "Sleep well and do not worry."

Clutching their own presents tightly, the tired children reluctantly took their parents' hands and went home. Fritz was sent straight to his room in disgrace, and Clara kissed her nutcracker gently and went to bed too.

HERR DROSSELMEYER
Unlike many sorcerers in ballet, Drosselmeyer (Stephen Wicks) makes wonderful things happen and performs only good deeds. In some productions, he becomes a Nutcracker Prince who partners Clara (Naomi Reynolds).

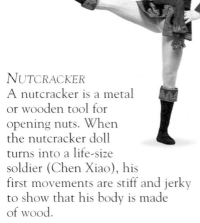

Clara puts her injured nutcracker to bed.

The wooden nutcracker

The adults dance while the children play.

Drosselmeyer surprises Clara with a gift chosen just for her.

NUTCRACKER
A nutcracker is a metal or wooden tool for opening nuts. When the nutcracker doll turns into a life-size soldier (Chen Xiao), his first movements are stiff and jerky to show that his body is made of wood.

✳

GRANDFATHER DANCE
One hundred years ago, the last group dance at German parties was the Grandfather Dance, which was the signal for the guests to go home. It also ends the festivities in this ballet.

The Nutcracker

BATTLE WITH THE MICE

♪ *MUSICAL NOTE*
As the Christmas tree grows taller and taller, the strings climb higher and higher, in a repeated pattern of rising notes. Brass instruments sound as the toy soldiers march into battle, and squeaking piccolos imitate the scurrying mice.

SWORDPLAY FOR SOLDIERS
Dancers fight duels in several ballets. Although the swords are not real, adults and children learn the correct way to use them so the fight scenes are both exciting and convincing. The soldier here is Mikhail Baryshnikov.

THE HOUSE WAS DARK and quiet when Clara tiptoed downstairs to make sure her nutcracker was safe. To her relief, he was exactly where she had left him, but the familiar room was mysteriously different. Long shadows slid across the floor, and the midnight chime of the grandfather clock echoed eerily.

All of a sudden the Christmas tree started to sway. Its fragile ornaments trembled, the tinsel shook, and slowly the tree grew taller and taller, until the top brushed the ceiling. Huddled beneath its heavy branches, Clara shivered with fright as the tree became a looming tower of winking lights.

"Perhaps I should go back to bed," she whispered to herself. Turning quickly, she saw a huge, angry mouse blocking her path, and more mice, with grasping paws and lashing tails, creeping towards her from all directions.

"Somebody help me," she cried.

An army of squealing mice follows the king into battle.

Clara has no chance to run and hide.

The cannon balls are made of solid sugar.

The Mouse King threatens the soldiers with his sharp claws.

Toy soldiers draw their swords to defend Clara.

At once, Fritz's tin soldiers snapped to attention and rushed to defend her. Then the Nutcracker leaped to his feet and charged into the battle, swinging his sword at the Mouse King.

Although he fought bravely, the Nutcracker soon stumbled under the king's ferocious attack. Desperate to save him, Clara took off her slipper and hurled it straight at the king. The startled mouse froze, and in that instant the Nutcracker killed him with one thrust of his sword.

The defeated mice slunk away, dragging their dead king after them. The Nutcracker vanished too, and Drosselmeyer's nephew appeared in his place, dressed as a prince. Placing the Mouse King's crown on Clara's head he led her away, into a whirlwind of glistening snow.

DANCE OF THE SNOWFLAKES
Spinning and sliding steps and sharply pointed patterns give the snowflake dance its shape and icy character. The dancers often move so quickly that their movements seem to fly in all directions, like real snow blown by the wind.

Clara and her prince venture into the snowy night.

Clara throws her slipper at the Mouse King.

The Nutcracker springs to life and attacks the Mouse King.

A PAIR OF STARS
The Nutcracker is the only famous ballet where children play the most important characters. Clara and Drosselmeyer's nephew (Petra Hoerrner and Victor Ostrovsky) can truly be called its heroine and hero.

The Nutcracker

THE LAND OF SWEETS

SUGAR PLUMS

SWEET SCENE
Inspired by the colours, shapes, and textures of real fruit and all sorts of sweets, each designer transforms the ballet's scenery and costumes into a luscious visual treat.

CANDY CANES

✳

JUMPING THROUGH HOOPS
In the original production of *The Nutcracker*, the dancers in the Russian dance, or *trepak*, were dressed as clowns. They carried hoops and jumped through them, as dancers still do today.

CLARA AND HER BRAVE young prince emerged from the snowstorm into a fantastic kingdom of sweets. They walked over butterscotch cobbles, past splashing fountains of lemonade and gleaming toffee pavilions, until they reached the transparent palace of the Sugar Plum Fairy.

"Thank you for coming to visit me," said the dainty fairy. Her tinkling voice rang like a cluster of silver bells. "Did you have a difficult journey?"

"We had to fight off the mice," Drosselmeyer's nephew explained. "I could not have beaten them alone, but Clara helped me by throwing her shoe at the Mouse King. Together we won the battle." Clara's face glowed with pleasure as he recounted the frightening

Everything in the Land of Sweets is made of sugar and spice.

Clara and Drosselmeyer's nephew are the honoured guests.

An Arabian dancer sways through the Coffee dance.

events. She was proud of her bravery, even though she did not say so.

"If you would like to rest here for a while, I will invite an assortment of my sweets to dance for you," said the Sugar Plum Fairy. She escorted the children to a splendid throne, where pages no bigger than elves offered them delicious cakes and cool drinks. Then, with a flourish of her wand, she summoned the entertainers.

First Chocolate slithered out of the crowd in a fiery Spanish dance that melted stamping feet and twisting shoulders into a creamy swirl.

Then the tantalizing figure of Arabian Coffee drifted by, floating in a cloud of veils as light and lacy as foam.

Chinese Tea burst into the hall like a stream of sunshine. Bubbling gaily, he bowed again and again to the children and the other guests.

Next in the parade of entertainers came the boisterous Russian peppermints, who tumbled head over heels past the throne, spraying slivers of energy everywhere.

A flock of marzipan shepherdesses followed them, bringing a touch of gentleness to the procession of tasty treats.

CHINESE STYLE
For more than 200 years, the same gestures have been used to define Chinese characters in ballet. Dancers bend their elbows, curl their hands into fists, and point their index fingers straight up.

✴

THE MIRLITONS
The shepherdesses' dance was originally named the Dance of the *Mirlitons*, which is French for "reed pipes". Sometimes the dancers pretend to play panpipes.

Candy cane columns

Chinese Tea

The arms curve in a graceful, inviting arc.

The Russians leap through their hoops.

Proud Spanish dancers represent Chocolate.

MIME: COME
The dancer lifts both arms in the same direction and rounds them gently, keeping the elbows down and the hands turned up. Then both arms are lowered and brought close to the body.

The Nutcracker

THE SUGAR PLUM FAIRY

♪ *MUSICAL NOTE*
The celesta, a type of keyboard instrument, was brand new when Tchaikovsky first heard it in Paris. He had one sent to him and introduced it to Russian music for the first time when he matched its light, sweet chime to the Sugar Plum Fairy's delicacy.

MOTHER GINGER
Originally named *Mère Gigogne* – the Old Woman Who Lived in a Shoe – this character is now often played by a man in an enormous hooped skirt. Children hide inside it when the character appears, and then burst out to dance.

✶

THE NOBLE PRINCE
The adult prince in the original production was called Koklush, a Russian version of the French word *coqueluche*, which means "whooping cough". His name has never been explained.

CLARA CLAPPED HER HANDS in glee and popped three jellybeans into her mouth. "Which dance did you like best?" she asked her prince. "Who do you think will appear next? I never knew the world could hold so much sweetness and so many surprises."

The boy smiled back at her, and she noticed the iced cakes had turned his mouth so red it looked like a cherry. Before he could reply, roly-poly Mother Ginger bustled into the hall, flapping her apron and herding all her children in front of her.

Soft and smooth as a pillow, she waited patiently while they romped and skipped around her.

A house made of toffee and licorice

The candied flowers form a pretty posy.

Children pop out from beneath Mother Ginger's huge skirt.

Mother Ginger glides among her frisky children, laughing merrily.

Then she flung her arms wide and gathered them up in a loving hug. They were still tickling one another and giggling with pleasure when she led them away.

In the hush they left behind them, a cascade of candied flowers danced across the glazed floor. Unfolding their gilded petals in overlapping waves, the blossoms swept through the hall, weaving intricate patterns around the spun-sugar columns and finally arranging themselves in a neat bouquet.

At last the Sugar Plum Fairy reappeared, with her own handsome prince by her side. Their elegant poise and gentle grace transformed their dance into a tender private conversation. When the fairy danced alone, she seemed to Clara like a delicate vision, as perfect as a beautiful dream.

"I want to be just like her when I grow up," Clara thought, "and I want every party to be as lively and pretty and happy as this one."

Stepping down from her throne, she kissed the Sugar Plum Fairy and thanked the entertainers. Then she took her prince's hand and they set off together to explore the future.

STEP: RETIRÉ
This French word means "withdrawn". To perform this step the dancer stands on a straight leg and bends the other leg so the knee points to the side and the toe points to the straight knee. The Sugar Plum Fairy (Agnes Oaks) often poses on one foot.

Clara and her prince wave goodbye to their new friends before they leave them forever.

The Sugar Plum Fairy scarcely touches the ground when she dances.

A HAPPY ENDING
Different productions end the ballet in different ways. Here, Clara (Megan Fairchild) rides into the future alone in a silver sleigh. Sometimes she wakes up in her own bed, believing her adventure was only a dream.

✳ Glossary ✳

CZARDAS IN *COPPÉLIA*

A

Act Principal divisions of the action of a ballet, separated by intervals/intermissions.

Adagio Musical term meaning "at ease" or "leisure". Slow and smooth movements.

Air, en l' In the air. An action of the working leg off the floor.

Arabesque Pose on one straight leg with working leg extended straight behind the body.

Assemblé Jump that brings two straight legs together in the air before a landing in fifth position.

Attitude Pose on one straight leg with working leg bent to the front, side, or back.

B

Ballerina From the Italian *ballare*, meaning "to dance". The highest rank of female dancer in the company.

Ballet Theatrical performance of group and solo dances that combines steps and music, often to tell a story.

Ballon Refers to the springiness of the feet and the bouncy quality of a dancer's jumps.

Barre Wooden railing attached to the studio wall to support dancers in the opening exercises of their daily lesson.

Battement, grand Large beating. A high kick of the straight leg to the front, side or back.

Battement, tendu Stretched beating. The working leg slides open to the front, side, or back – with the toe resting lightly on the floor – and then closes again.

Beat To strike the legs together in the air before completing a jump.

Bolero Lively Spanish dance in triple time, often accompanied by castanets.

Bourrée A series of small, even running steps in fifth position, performed quickly and lightly. The front foot advances, and the back foot catches up with it.

Bras Arm or arms.

C

Cabriole Jump where one leg kicks up, to the front, side, or back, and the other rises to meet it in the air.

Caractère Character. Describes roles that require acting and mime gestures but few classical steps.

Centre work The second part of a ballet class, after the barre exercises, in which the dancers work in the centre of the room without support.

Changement Jump from fifth position to fifth position, in which the feet change place in the air.

Choreographer The person who chooses and arranges the steps of a ballet.

Choreography The arrangement of the steps in a ballet.

Classical ballet Work based on the traditional technique that developed from 17th century court dancing.

Corps de ballet Body of the ballet. The dancers in a company who perform as a group framing the solo dancers and enhancing the atmosphere.

Czardas Lively Hungarian folk dance.

D

Danseur Male dancer.

Danseur, premier First dancer. The leading male dancer.

Décor The scenery and costumes for a ballet.

Demi Half. A small position.

Développé Developing movement. The working leg unfolds gradually after it leaves the floor until it is straight at its greatest height.

Divertissement Diversion. The dances that show off the dancers' skill and grace without advancing the story.

E

Échappé An escaping step. A jump where the feet begin in a closed position and separate in the air before landing apart.

Elevation Refers to a dancer's ability to jump high.

Ensemble Together. The entire company or the *corps de ballet* as a unit.

Entrechat Jump that begins and ends in fifth position, with the feet crisscrossing several times in the air.

Épaulement The graceful placing of the head, neck, and shoulders.

F

Fermé Closed. A movement that ends with the feet together.

Flies The area above the stage in which scenery painted on cloth is stored until needed.

Flying The raising of scenery above the stage. Also, the movement of dancers through the air on wires.

Folk dancing Native dances of any country used as part of a ballet.

G

Glissade Gliding step, done in any direction.

Grand Big. A big movement.

Grand pas de deux An important dance for the ballerina and her partner. It usually contains a slow opening duet, solos for each dancer, and a rapid closing duet.

J

Jambe Leg.

Jambe, rond de Circular leg movement, either on the ground or in the air.

Jeté Thrown. A jump from one foot to the other.

Jeté, petit Small jump that quickly shifts the weight from one foot to the other.

Jeté, grand Big jump that throws the body through the air.

L

Leotard Skintight garment, with or without sleeves and legs, worn for class and rehearsals.

Line The dancer's outline when the body is moving or stationary.

M

Mark To sketch or indicate a movement in class or rehearsal.

Matinée An afternoon performance.

Mazurka Polish folk dance with three strong beats, filled with foot-stamping and heel-clicking.

Mime The use of arm and hand gestures to represent words. The gestures follow the order of words in a French sentence.

N, O

Notation Writing down movement in symbols rather than words.

Ouvert Open. A movement that ends with the feet apart.

Overture The music before the rise of the curtain and the first appearance of the dancers.

P

Pas Step.

Pas de chat Step of the cat. A light high jump. One foot after the other is pulled very close to the body.

Pas de deux Any dance for two.

Pas de trois Dance for three.

Pas de quatre Dance for four.

Petit Small. A small movement.

Pirouette One or more turns on one spot with the working foot pointing to the knee of the supporting leg.

Plié Bending. Where one or both knees bend outwards, over the toes.

Pointe shoe Woman's shoe with a stiffened toe on which the dancer stands. Also called a toe shoe.

Port de bras The carriage of the arms. The placing of the arms in relation to the head and body.

Prologue An introduction to the main action. The opening act of *The Sleeping Beauty* is called the Prologue.

R

Relevé Raised. Raising the body by lifting the heels off the floor.

Romantic ballet Works created in the early 19th century that contrast reality with fantasy through stories of men in love with spirits.

Rosin A powder dancers use on their shoes to stop them from slipping during a performance.

S

Saut Jump from two feet that ends with the feet in the original position.

Sauté Jumped. Any movement to which a hop is added.

Scene Short portion of an act, marked by the appearance of additional characters or by a change of location.

Scenery The furniture and painted cloths that establish the time and place of the action.

Solo Dance for one.

Soubrette Spirited female dancer with bubbly charm and a talent for comic acting.

Spotting The practice of whipping the head around while turning to avoid getting dizzy.

Stage left To the left of the dancer on the stage.

Stage right To the right of the dancer on the stage.

Supporting leg The leg supporting the body's weight while the other leg is off the floor.

T

Tendu Stretched. See *Battement, tendu*.

Terre, à On the ground. An action of the working leg on the floor.

Terre à terre Ground to ground. Steps that leave the floor only briefly, as opposed to jumps.

Tour A turn of the body.

Tour en l'air Complete turn of the body in the air.

Travesti, en Refers to a female dancer playing the part of a man.

Turnout Basic rule of classical dance that requires the knees to turn away from each other at all times.

Tutu, classical Woman's costume, tightly fitted around the body and waist, with a stiff frill for the skirt.

Tutu, Romantic Woman's costume, tightly fitted around the body, with a calf-length, gauzy skirt.

V, W

Variation Solo dance.

Waltz Dance in triple time or based on the count of three.

Working leg The leg that performs a movement while the other leg supports the weight of the body.

A *PAS DE DEUX* FROM *SWAN LAKE*

✳ *Index* ✳

ACKNOWLEDGEMENTS
The publishers would like to thank the following:
Coral Mula for illustrations on pp 8-9; Michael
Johnstone for advice on music; Porselli Dance Wear in
Covent Garden, London, for the loan of leotards and
tights; Dr Giannandrea Poesio for guidance with mime
gestures; Margaret Barbieri from the London Studio
Centre, and students Amy Bailey, Anthony Gordon,
Michelle McGuire and Juan Rodriguez; The Royal
Ballet School; Royal Academy of Dancing library; Lynn
Bressler for the index; Andy Crawford at the DK studio

PICTURE CREDITS
Key: t = top, b = bottom, c = centre, l = left, r = right
Catherine Ashmore: (English National Ballet) 52-53;
Atlanta Ballet 55cr;
Paul de Backer: (Royal Ballet of Flanders) 22-23, 38tl;
Patrick Baldwin: (English National Ballet) 29cr;
Bridgeman Art Library/Walter Hussey Bequest: 18cr;
J. L. Charmet: 28tl;
Dee Conway: (English National Ballet) 16tl, (Kirov
Ballet) 24tl, (Moscow City Ballet) 21tr, (The Royal

Ballet) 13tr, 21cr, 25tr, 25br, 55tr;
Bill Cooper: (English National Ballet) 10-11;
Costas: (New York City Ballet/George Balanchine's *The
Nutcracker* © The George Balanchine Trust) 54cl, 57br,
60tl;
Anthony Crickmay: 7bl, 7c, 7tr;
Zoe Dominic: 15tr, (English National Ballet) 44tl;
Richard Farley: (English National Ballet) 47br;
Sean Hudson: (Scottish Ballet) 49tr;
Hulton-Getty Picture Collection: 7tl, 26tl, 38bl, 50tl;
Robbie Jack: (The Royal Ballet) 7br, (Houston Ballet)
47cr;
Rolf Kay: (Ballet West) 61br;
Paul Kolnik: (New York City Ballet/*The Sleeping Beauty*
choreographed by Peter Martins - after Marius Petipa)
18br, (New York City Ballet/*Coppélia*, choreography by
George Balanchine © The George Balanchine Trust)
35tr, 36tl, 37cr, 40tl, 41tr;
Gustaaf Lauwers: (Royal Ballet of Flanders) 29tr;
Lelli & Masotti, Archivo Fotografico, Corpo di Ballo
del Teatro alla Scala: 46tl, 49br;
Nan Melville: (The Royal Ballet) 14bl, (Kirov Ballet)

27tr, (Pennsylvania Ballet) 57tr;
Mira: (American Ballet Theatre) 45tr;
*Musée de Neuilly/Musée de la Femme et Collection
d'Automates*/Photo: J.P. Stercq· 37cr;
Marty Sohl: (San Francisco Ballet - Tomasson's
Swan Lake after Petipa/Ivanov) 47tr;
Leslie E. Spatt: (Australian Ballet) 39tr, 40bl, (Kirov
Ballet) 17tr, 31tr;
Angela Taylor: (Australian Ballet) 27br, (Birmingham
Royal Ballet) 59tr, (English National Ballet) 61tr, (The
Royal Ballet) 20tl, 30tl;
Peter Teigen: (London City Ballet) 32-33, 36bl,
42-43, 48tl;
© **Jack Vartoogian**: (American Ballet Theatre) 34bl,
50cl, 56cl, (Dance Theatre of Harlem) 51tr, (Royal
Danish Ballet) 34tl.

Every effort has been made to trace the copyright
holders and we apologize in advance for any
unintentional omissions. We would be pleased to insert
the appropriate acknowledgement in any subsequent
edition of this publication.